GIANT SHORT-FACED BEARS

by Sara Gilbert

CREATIVE EDUCATION • CREATIVE PAPERBACKS

Published by Creative Education and Creative Paperbacks
P.O. Box 227, Mankato, Minnesota 56002
Creative Education and Creative Paperbacks are
imprints of **The Creative Company**
www.thecreativecompany.us

Design and production by **Chelsey Luther**
Art direction by **Rita Marshall**
Printed in the **United States of America**

Photographs by Alamy (Chronicle, Nadezda Murmakova, patchanu noree,
Stocktrek Images, Inc.), Dreamstime (Artesiawells, Nicolas Fernandez, Tranac),
FreeVectorMaps.com, Science Source (Gary Hincks, Mark Hallett Paleoart)

Illustration on cover and p. 1 © **2016** Kelly Taylor

Library of Congress Cataloging-in-Publication Data
Gilbert, Sara.
Giant short-faced bears / Sara Gilbert.
p. cm. — (Ice age mega beasts)
Includes bibliographical references and index.
Summary: An elementary exploration of giant short-faced bears, focusing on
fossil evidence that helps explain how their long legs and wide snouts helped
these beasts adapt to the last Ice Age.

ISBN 978-1-60818-766-9 (hardcover)
ISBN 978-1-62832-374-0 (pbk)
ISBN 978-1-56660-808-4 (eBook)
1. Giant short-faced bear—Juvenile literature. 2. Bears, Fossil—Juvenile literature. 3. Mammals, Fossil—Juvenile literature. 4. Prehistoric animals.

QE882.C15 G54 2017
569.78—dc23   2016014624

CCSS: RI.1.1, 2, 3, 4, 5, 6, 7, 10; RI.2.1, 2, 4, 5, 6, 7, 10; RI.3.1, 2, 4, 5, 7, 10;
RF.1.1, 2, 3, 4; RF.2.3, 4; RF.3.3, 4

First Edition HC 9 8 7 6 5 4 3 2 1
First Edition PBK 9 8 7 6 5 4 3 2 1

Contents

Sleeping Giant

It's dark and quiet in the cave. Outside, a river runs through the woods. Inside, a giant short-faced bear is resting.

Many bears today rest in caves or other hidden places during winter.

The giant short-faced bear was bigger than today's bears. It stood almost 12 feet (3.7 m) tall. Its sharp claws could reach up to scratch cave walls 15 feet (4.6 m) high!

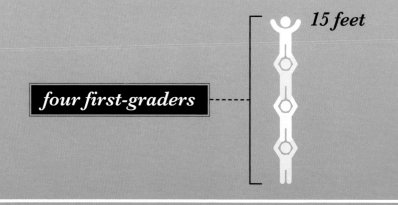

15 feet

four first-graders

Bears that lived long ago have left scratch marks and paw prints in caves.

Bears of the Ice Age

Giant short-faced bears roamed North America a million years ago. They lived during the last Ice Age. Northern lands were covered by huge sheets of ice. These were called glaciers.

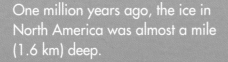

Ice Age glaciers

One million years ago, the ice in North America was almost a mile (1.6 km) deep.

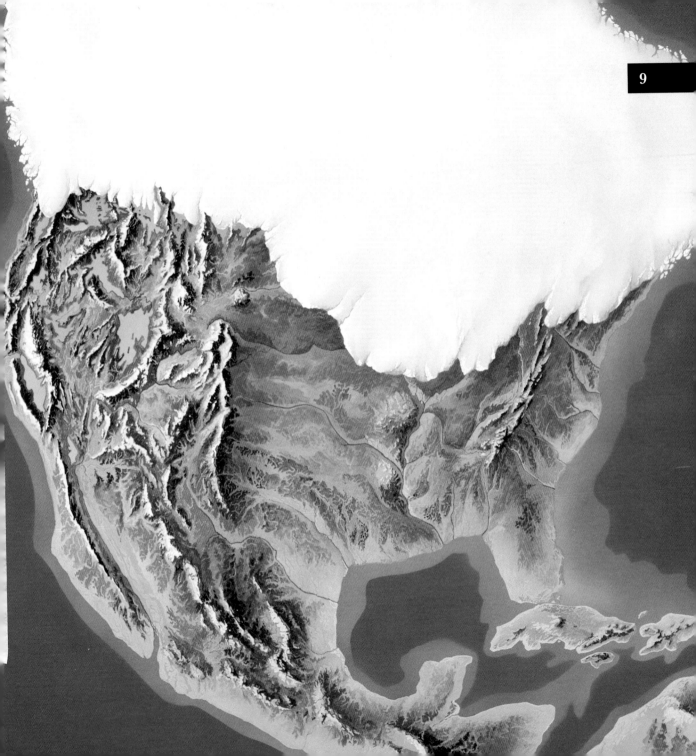

The huge bears scared off other *predators*. Fierce dire wolves left their kills behind when they saw bears. Then the bears ate the meat.

Animals that eat food others have left behind are called scavengers.

North American Home

The bears lived in thick forests and on open grasslands. Sometimes, they built *dens* in caves near rivers and lakes.

Other prehistoric bears, like cave bears, lived in the forests and caves of Europe.

The first complete *skeleton* was found in Indiana in 1967. Scientists got excited about that. They have learned a lot from *fossils*.

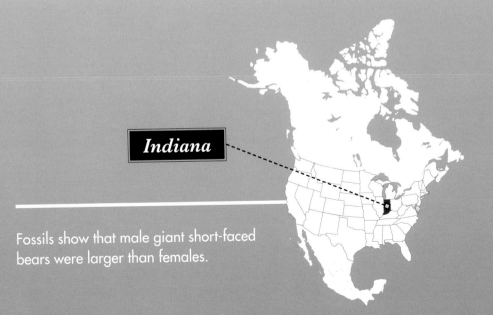

Indiana

Fossils show that male giant short-faced bears were larger than females.

Carnivorous Chasers

The giant short-faced bear was one of the biggest Ice Age *carnivores*. Its long legs helped it run after animals.

12 feet

Giant short-faced bears may have been able to run more than 40 miles (64.4 km) per hour.

The bear had a wide snout. Its nose and mouth were huge. Its teeth were strong and sharp. It could crush bones with a single bite!

The giant short-faced bear is also known as the bulldog bear for its wide snout.

The Earth got too warm for enormous animals when the Ice Age ended. They couldn't find enough food to survive. Giant short-faced bears died out about 10,000 years ago.

Some scientists think giant short-faced bears ate plants, too.

Giant Short-faced Bear Close-up

fur

snout

teeth

legs

claws

Glossary

carnivores: animals that eat meat

dens: hidden homes of some wild animals

fossils: remains of animals or plants

predators: animals that hunt other animals for food

skeleton: the bones inside an animal's body

Read More

Goecke, Michael P. *Short-Faced Bear.* Edina, Minn.: Abdo, 2004.

Turner, Alan. *National Geographic Prehistoric Mammals.* Washington, D.C.: National Geographic, 2004.

Websites

Enchanted Learning: Ice Age Mammals
http://www.enchantedlearning.com/subjects /mammals/Iceagemammals.shtml
Find out more about the Ice Age and the animals that lived then.

University of Iowa Museum of Natural History: Giant Short-faced Bear
http://mnh.uiowa.edu/giant-short-faced-bear
Read about the discovery of giant short-faced bear fossils in Iowa in 2008.

Note: Every effort has been made to ensure that the websites listed above are suitable for children, that they have educational value, and that they contain no inappropriate material. However, because of the nature of the Internet, it is impossible to guarantee that these sites will remain active indefinitely or that their contents will not be altered.

Index